MW01223707

What
LOVE
Does

OTHER BOOKS BY THE AUTHOR

The Future of Democracy:
Lessons from the Past and Present to
Guide Us on Our Path Forward

The Death of Democracy

Truth & Democracy

Everyday Spirituality for Everyone

Guide to Living in a Democracy

The Pursuit of Happiness

What LOVE Does

by

Steve Zolno

REGENT PRESS
Berkeley, California
2024

Copyright © 2024 by Steve Zolno

paperback:
ISBN 13: 978-1-58790-685-5
ISBN 10: 1-58790-685-6

e-book:
ISBN 13: 978-1-58790-686-2
ISBN: 10: 1-58790-686-4

Library of Congress Control Number: 2024907357

Cover Image:
"Ring of Fire" Solar Eclipse, October 14, 2023

Manufactured in the U.S.A.
Regent Press
Berkeley, California
www.regentpress.net
regentpress@mindspring.com

*Dedicated To
The Loving Place
Within Each Of Us*

CONTENTS

Love is the God of Peace
– FROM *Anacréon* BY RAMEAU

1. INTRODUCTION

Love is the predominant force in our lives from the time we are born.

We enter this world feeling at one with all that surrounds us — an experience of connection and love. But that feeling fades as we begin to think of ourselves as separate from others and the world.

Deep within we maintain a memory of that feeling and continually seek to reawaken it. We usually pursue it indirectly, hoping for others or the world to bring it to us. The direct way is allowing it to ourselves regardless of the circumstances of our lives.

That feeling seeks to emerge within each of us in this moment — and every moment — as does the sun during an eclipse. We give it many names: joy, happiness, recognition, connection, peace of mind, freedom, nurturance, forgiveness, compassion, kindness, appreciation, and others.

What blocks that feeling is our thoughts about the past, our judgment of the present and our worries about the future. Love may focus on a person, place, or object, but it actually is a feeling independent of them we can allow ourselves. And as we do this it opens our eyes, our minds, and our hearts.

Our priority is meeting our basic needs. Beyond that whatever we do — and wherever we go — it is our quest for love that guides us. Love assures us we are on a viable path in our pursuit of understanding, friendships, relationships, work or career, and even our recreational activities. When lacking that feeling we are less confident in ourselves and the direction of our lives.

When felt, love affects all levels of our being. It is mental, physical, and emotional at the same time. We allow it to ourselves when we feel it from another or when the universe seems to confirm our value by our getting what we want. But soon that feeling fades and we are left seeking it once again. We usually think of love as a goal for the future rather than allowing ourselves to experience it in the present.

Throughout childhood most of us receive love that contributes to our growth and development; at first unconditionally from our mothers, then conditionally from our fathers. We return to our mothers to reassure us of our value. Our fathers shape our actions by expecting more for their approval as we mature. But these roles are not static; mothers and fathers can provide unconditional or conditional love. Single parents must balance both roles, and others can be parent surrogates. All parents, being humans who struggle to lead their own lives, at times are imperfect and inconsistent in their roles and duties to their children.

Love is our most essential nature that we sacrifice on the altar of everyday living. But that feeling can be resurrected at any moment we decide to bring it back into our lives. As we do this, we gain more confidence to move through our daily struggles.

We spend our lives looking for love — at times in the right places and at times in the wrong ones. In our quest we often fail to differentiate between the best and worst sources — especially as children. We absorb views and attitudes toward others and the world from those close to us or other models. We learn whether the world is a safe place and if people are to be trusted.

For those who fail to get emotional support, it is lack of love that may shape their views and actions. But no one experiences perfect nurturance and guidance. We all emerge with doubts and fears about our abilities and value, and continue to seek confirmation of our worth throughout our lives.

Love recognizes the uniqueness of every individual. It affirms the value of all human beings, including those of every race, gender, religion, sexual orientation, social standing, those with disabilities and various maladies, even those who have harmed people and need to be kept from others.

There is a myth in our society — and every society — that what we do, or what happens to us, or what others do to us determines our value as a person. But our essential nature never changes: we always have been and always will be worthy of love. When we look beyond the façade people present to the world we see that with greater clarity.

As we extend love to others, we experience it for ourselves. As we deny it to others, we also deny it to ourselves. As we bring it into our activities it transforms them and us.

We continually look outside ourselves for permission to experience love, but only we can allow it to ourselves, and only in this moment. Despite what we have been taught or come to believe, there is nothing we need do to become worthy of love. No self-improvement can bring it to us, only a willingness to experience it.

The idea that there is something we can or must do to get what we most want is what keeps love from us. If in this moment we simply choose to acknowledge the feeling we seek, it will reemerge. And we can allow ourselves that experience in the next moment, and then the next.

We never can force love to emerge, we only can move out of its way and allow it to come forth. As we experience it there is no hurry; each moment is cherished and enjoyed. Even when experiencing unhappiness we can begin to allow ourselves love, which slowly transforms our mood and view of the world.

In each moment — including this one — we choose love or blame. With blame we hurt ourselves and may or may not affect anyone else; with love we have what we most want regardless of its effect on others. You may tell yourself you can't experience the feeling you seek right now because circumstances aren't right — your past controls you or the world is too full of hate or you don't deserve it or someone is keeping it from you. Circumstances always will provide a reason to deny ourselves love if that is where we choose to focus.

When we perpetually put off the feeling we want for the future, that future never comes. But it actually is our mindset that holds us back. We all have the potential for love within us and can allow it to ourselves in this moment if we choose.

Our descriptions of love are composed of words, but they only point to it. When we look inside we find that love is our most essential self that dwells within us in a place beyond words.

Everything we do in our interactions with others — and even with objects — we can do lovingly. We can connect to the inside of a person rather just observing from the outside. We can interact from a stance of understanding rather than judgment, including our interactions with ourselves. This brings us the experience of understanding we seek.

We have learned to process our perceptions of others — and ourselves — through our thoughts and to leave out the feeling of connection we once had. The experience of love makes us fully human once again. It restores the most essential part we left behind. It calms the body, mind and soul. It brings our awareness more fully into the present.

Our education usually fails to teach us the essential skills of recognizing the value of others and working together to resolve issues, so very few of us possess those capabilities.

The vast majority of information we receive from our media and entertainment focuses on what is wrong or missing in our world. It informs us that there always is much strife and little hope. It teaches us that problems must be dealt with by confrontation or violence, and provides no model for how to resolve issues without them. It fails to impart a vision of how to move toward a better world.

The pages that follow provide a guide for how love can be brought back into our lives and interactions. If we choose, we can use that knowledge to move closer to the world we envision. But that depends on us taking responsibility for going beyond being victims of our circumstances. It begins by reigniting what we most want in our lives and then infusing that into every realm of our experience.

Are you free of others' opinions of you?
Are you free of your opinion of yourself?
– MARLON BRANDO[1]

2. THE SELF

Our self is the filter through which we experience everything and everyone.

We are born with a sense of connection to all that surrounds us. We then begin to develop concepts of ourselves, others and the world, and live our lives based on those images.[2] The young child alternates between a sense of connection to the world and separateness. That gradually yields to a belief that we are separate beings. Then for the remainder of our lives we seek to return to that original sense of connection.

At first our ideas about ourselves are influenced by those around us who, for most of us, convey that we are loved no matter what we do. This assurance guides us through our early years as we experiment by trial and error to learn about the world. Some parents fail to provide adequate nurturance which instills doubt, including the child's idea of whether he or she is lovable

Eventually our views are influenced by the media, entertainment sources, reading, and reflecting on what we see and hear.

Children's bodies reflect their developing idea of who they are. Physical looseness gradually yields to a more solid sense of self, which they convey to the world by how they walk, talk and carry themselves.

Regardless of the amount of support we are provided as children, we spend our lives wondering if we are worthy of love. We seek reassurance from others in the hope they will affirm our value. We try to boost our self-esteem by participation in skills development, financial pursuits, or competition.

Our minds are not separate from our bodies and emotions. Every thought is felt, sometimes generally and sometimes in specific areas where we experience joy or pain. In recent years functional MRI's have confirmed this, but we don't need them to verify what we already know from self-observation.[3]

The concepts we develop about ourselves, others and the world always are incomplete. Life continually surprises us. The "real world" remains elusive even as we participate in interactions that seem real. Yet some people develop belief systems that cause them to think they have the truth and become unwilling to open to information that may contradict what they already think they know.

Our minds only can process a limited amount of information at one time. We often see one side of a situation and miss all the rest. That is why we need to go beyond our usual thought process for real understanding.

We seem different to different people, and our self-image varies from one time to the next. A parent, teacher, or friend may convey that we are intelligent and competent, while others may see us lacking those qualities. Judgments may be communicated verbally or by body language, such as a smile or disapproving look. As we internalize the input of others we consider ourselves more worthy of love at times and less worthy at other times.

As we inject the judgments of others into our minds they also affect our bodies. Our posture conveys more confidence or less, depending on what we internalize. We are more relaxed when feeling loved and more tense when feeling judged. When feeling loved we move in a manner that is loose and relaxed. It can be seen and felt in how we walk and talk; we are more comfortable expressing our creative side. Our

breathing also reflects whether we feel connected and loved. It flows easily when we are
comfortable, but often we are unaware of how
we fail to breathe when we experience discomfort or a threat.[4] We can hold on to memories of
traumatic events for years.[5]

Being human, we go through the gamut of
emotions that flesh is heir to: happiness, peace,
love and self-esteem alternate with anger, sadness, jealousy, and self-judgment. Most of us
have the same standards for ourselves we have
for others, which often leads to thinking that we
or our actions are inadequate. We may even hate
ourselves at times. We blame people for making
us look bad or depriving us of love, but actually it is our own lack of belief in our worthiness
that keeps the experience of love from us.[6]

We do this while putting on a façade of being
consistent individuals with stable feelings and
moods. This is common even among those we
consider the most consistent and accomplished.[7]
But inside we know that an unpredictable wave
of feeling can rise up and threaten to wash over
us at any time.

We spend our lives hoping that people and
circumstances will meet our expectations, but it
seems they always fall short. Our frustrations
mount as others and the world fail us and we

find them unworthy of our love. But doing that also deprives us of the feeling we most want.

We are destined to go through the gamut of human experience — love and hate, fulfillment and disappointment — repeatedly. But despite our descent into discontent and despair, there is a way to reclaim our sense of connection and love. We can begin by recognizing we are the monsters of our own creation. When willing to admit — if only to ourselves — we are uncomfortable in our skin due to our habit of judging the world, others and ourselves, we can begin to evoke the sense of forgiveness we once called upon our parents to provide.

The alternative to forgiveness is chronic anger and judgment. This has resulted in the self-destructive behavior of many who have reached the pinnacle of fame and fortune only to realize that — despite being worshipped by others — they bring their judgmental selves with them wherever they go and are unable to escape the torment that comes from their internal critical voice.

A danger here is thinking we "should" forgive ourselves which is just another form of self-judgment. The experience of forgiveness is different from the thought. So we might ask ourselves "what does forgiveness feel like?" As experienced, it really is another form of love.

The most important skill we can learn is to allow ourselves that feeling of forgiveness. We consistently find another reason not to do this. But whatever you're thinking, whatever you're feeling, and whatever you have done, you can forgive yourself if you choose. The more willing you are to bring forgiveness to yourself, the less likely you will repeat angry acts you may regret.

We are the only species that have long-term expectations for ourselves and our society. Planning our future has allowed us to create the civilizations with which we have covered the earth. But we also are caught in an endless pursuit of perfection where we judge our progress against expectations we fail to meet. We continually internalize the conflict between the ideal world in which we want to live and the one in which we actually dwell.

That conflict is the force that has projected us forward as we have tried to move toward a vision of what our society should look like. We chronically complain about the state of our world. We sense there is something missing but are unsure about what we want instead. We are certain that things should be different while unable to clarify how the society we want should look.

We can see that children have moods that

fluctuate between high and low, rationality and irrationality, mental presence and absence, and we usually are willing to forgive them. When we take an honest look at ourselves and others we see that our moods also fluctuate regardless of circumstances. Yet we blame the conditions around us and put our hope for fulfillment on the expectation they will improve. Alternately we may become depressed by believing there is no hope. What we go through is an essential part of being human, but always expecting things to be different sets us up for perpetual disappointment. To get rid of our fluctuations would be to eliminate an essential part of who we are. Situations and people don't make us depressed; rather, we make ourselves depressed by our expectation that we and our lives should be different.

Sometimes a feeling of isolation comes upon us for no known reason. It drags us away from our connection to events and people. It is a place where our minds decide they must go for as long as it takes. We should know there is nothing wrong with us even in the deepest throes of depression. All we really can do is allow ourselves the time and space we need to move through it. The support and understanding of others may help, but the only way out is through it at the pace it chooses.

Does that mean we should lack empathy for those who are depressed? Just the opposite — depression is the result of feeling alone with our burden. Those under its influence may need support to allow their inner ogre the compassion it needs to stop torturing its victims. At such times having someone to bear witness to our process can be helpful. Hopefully not to repeat our theme too often, but regardless of what others do, ultimately only we can allow the experience of love and nurturance to ourselves.

Babies cry for what seems like no reason. Adult moods also swing for what seems like no reason. This contradicts our assumption about the consistency of the human personality. Mood changes are normal and our expectation of consistency is very much a myth. Altering our perspective allows us to experience the world from both a connected and unconnected view; both are needed for balanced functioning. But allowing ourselves love can guide us through our best and worst moments — including this one — if we let it.

We hold standards for ourselves that are impossible to meet. We have ideals about how we should act, how we should be consistent, and how our bodies should look or feel, but the reality nearly always differs from what we expect. Regardless of our self-doubt, our lives call for consistency; we need to show up and follow through with our family, school, work and friends.

Yet there is a part of us we often forget. It is the part that — much like the ideal parent — nurtures us even with the unexpected feelings that threaten to overwhelm us at times. It is the part that allows us to be who we are with all our inconsistencies. It supports us even as we falter. As we evoke that part of us we allow ourselves love in this moment regardless of the vicissitudes of our minds.

We think we will be happy when we get what we want — when we or our team wins, when we have enough money, when we fall in love. But the key to happiness is not having everything go our way. Rather, it is acknowledging we have limited control over events and our reactions to those events. When we stop trying to make ourselves and the world meet our expectations we become more willing to go with the hand we are dealt.

This doesn't mean we stop setting goals and trying to reach them. Humans have succeeded — to this point — because of their ability to plan the future and execute their plans. But our efforts often come up short of expectation and always will.

Rather than holding out for perfection, we can enjoy the pursuit of our vision. We can allow love into our lives right now regardless of whether our standards are met. As we do this we experience the fulfillment we hoped our expectations would bring. We then can take that feeling into whatever we do as we realize that getting what we think we want fails to provide the fulfillment we really want. And as we begin to bring the feeling of love into our everyday interactions it transforms them.

When the world fails our expectations we can fight for our vision, and at times we may need to do so. But being in a constant struggle works against us by putting us in a chronic fight/flight mode that keeps us from our ultimate goal of fulfillment. And even if the world were to meet our expectations, would we be content or would we continue to focus on its shortcomings to justify our dissatisfaction?

So how do we deal with the disappointment and anger that wells up when others or the world fail us, or when we just feel angry for an unknown reason? There are those who say we have no control over our emotions, and there are those who say we can control them. They both are right.

We all have negative reactions to events at times. They are unlikely to go away. We assume our suffering is caused by others or the circumstances of our lives. We may think our discomfort is the result of a difficult past we carry with us.[8] But our past cannot determine what we do in the present. What's most important for the quality of our lives is not what happens to us, but what we do with what happens to us.

Regardless of the past, which includes all time up until the present, we can choose to bring the experience of love back into our lives by evoking it in this moment. If your mind is focused on your shortcomings or those of the world, you can ask yourself if you want to continue to dwell there, or if you want to allow yourself an experience of acceptance and love. You can directly bring that feeling to yourself rather than waiting for the world to bring it to you. In each moment we choose to focus on the past and our worries about the future, or the quality of our lives in the present.

But we cannot have the experience we seek unless open to it. Regardless of how well things go or how wonderful our lives look from the outside, we don't necessarily experience fulfillment. So you might ask yourself what is love and what does it feel like? As you take the time to answer that question — not necessarily verbally — you may find yourself becoming more relaxed and breathing more deeply. You might find that you feel less hostile or threatened by the world. Give yourself a few moments to stabilize that feeling. Once secure, you can bring it into the next moment and the next. Every situation might not be right for experiencing love, but it is possible to bring it into the vast majority of circumstances. *if priveleged*

From the vantage of love, everything looks different. We no longer expect it to be granted to us but become secure in allowing it to ourselves. We no longer need the world or others or ourselves to meet our expectations; we see them more realistically and forgivingly, with their faults and beauty. We bring a new appreciation to all we encounter.

Love allows us to see who and what is around us more realistically when we're not stuck on them taking a particular form. But we tend to convert our insights into concepts we think always will be valid. Just because you have brought yourself an experience of love doesn't mean you can create a formula that will work for all time. Bringing the feeling we want into the moment consists of an openness and flexibility to the continually changing conditions within us and without.

It is a custom, especially in the Western world, to believe that thinking is the route to

all progress. It may be true that the innate intelligence of every human being is the driving
force behind our efforts to identify and work
toward a sense of fulfillment. Real intelligence
understands that what we ultimately seek is
love on a feeling level. Real intelligence never _vocab?_
can be mechanical or artificial — regardless of
the advancement of technology — because it
includes a reflection on our pursuit of a purpose
in life. It involves us at a feeling, as well as a
thinking, level.

  Our ultimate goal is the inner peace that love
brings. Once having experienced that, it often
slips away because we turn it into a thought.
But no amount of thinking can bring us what
we most want. Seeing the limits of our thought
process is a first step.

  It is common to be caught in chronic criticism
where nothing and no one lives up to our ideals.
But that has little to do with the real world and
much to do with our ingrained fault-finding, by
which we mainly hurt ourselves.

  Love brings a sense of appreciation to all our
interactions. When we simply observe others
and the world around us — rather than dwelling
on their shortcomings — we can allow that feeling of appreciation to emerge. There always is a
need to improve the world, but we can focus on

that without blaming or harming anyone. The reality of who we are vastly exceeds our idea of ourselves. It includes our infinite potential as well as our imperfections. And as we recognize the complex and unpredictable nature of other human beings we bring that same recognition to ourselves.

We can be caught in anger or resentment toward those we believe fail to understand us. But this hurts us and may not affect anyone else. And telling ourselves that negative feelings are bad only adds to them. Identifying the direction we want to go — which always is toward the experience of love — and allowing it to ourselves is the only real way forward.

vs the present

The same is true for pain, both mental and physical. When we fight pain we make it worse. Our first reaction often is tension and withholding our breath. We usually can reduce pain when we no longer fight it, when we allow ourselves to relax and breathe to the extent possible. As we fully experience pain or discomfort it may seem to get worse before it gets better. The best way out is through it — guided by the love and compassion that only we can bring to ourselves.

meditation

Despite our efforts to maintain a consistent appearance, our minds sometimes take off in directions we barely recognize. This is confirmation that our true nature is not a consistent being, but a composite of elements that at times seem like they don't belong in a single self. The reality is that we're often inconsistent and illogical, which is a truer model of who we are than the façade of consistency we present to the world. Our sanity depends on a willingness to embrace the irrational — as well as the rational — reality of who we are.

When we allow ourselves love, the diversions of our minds no longer are fearful, but become an expression of the multiple and creative sides with which we once were comfortable. We tried to close them off as they threatened our self-image of consistent and unified individuals. But no one is of a single mind, and love allows us to acknowledge — and as appropriate — express all sides of ourselves as they come to the surface. This also is the way that art and music give expression to the nonverbal side of us.

The world around us, as well as our inner world, always will remain unpredictable. On the inside — as well as the outside — we often seem inconsistent and contradictory. But as we acknowledge the fluctuations that constitute our everyday reality they seem less threatening. What upsets us is not the roller coaster of reality, but our expectation of consistency. Bringing love — rather than fear — to our experience allows us to encounter our fluctuations as the normal course of events they really are.

There always have been disasters as well as reasons to celebrate. There are terrible events and joyous moments where our minds can dwell. But in this moment we can choose to focus on incidents from the past that attempt to impose themselves on our minds or on the task and situation before us.

Our actions are based on views we hold about others and the world. We rarely stop to examine our beliefs or compare them with the reality in front of us. We go around at least partially blinded. Yet if we were to continually stop to examine all our actions we probably would get very little done. The advancement of civilization — and the progress of our views and comfort with the world around us — require a willingness to continually open our eyes and see the world anew. This brings us greater peace of mind as our views become more aligned with reality.

Most of us are thoroughly entrenched in the land of "should." We chronically think we must improve ourselves and our lives. We continually create resolutions: "I should lose weight, I should get more exercise, I should treat people better, I shouldn't trust people." We assume that if we comply with an elusive ideal of how we think we should act it will enhance our self-esteem and experience of love. When we see that we are doing that we may be able to curb the habit for a while. But if we convert that insight into another "should," we are back where we started. As we become aware of how we habitually sacrifice our peace of mind and self-esteem in the present for a future when we hope things will be better, we begin to understand that the future never comes. It only is in this moment we can allow ourselves the love we seek without turning it into another "should."

In a very real way there is more than one self that dwells within us. We often are undecided — or even at war with ourselves — about the correct way to act: "Shall I forgo that extra helping?" "Shall I get up and do my exercises?" "Shall I seek revenge against that person who insulted me?" By using functional MRI technology, neuroscientists have shown that our mental functions are accompanied by stimulation to regions of our brain. A part of our brain (the autonomic system) is involved in actions and responses to the world. Another part (the cerebral cortex) consciously governs what we do, like when we tell our legs or arms to move. Yet another (the prefrontal cortex) guides us to

make decisions based on what we have learned.[9]
Hormones also are released with our experience
of emotion, such as oxytocin with love, and tes-
tosterone with aggression. Different parts of
ourselves often are in conflict with each other,
setting up a moral dilemma when we are undecided about the right way to act. What feels like
inner conflict is not just present in our thoughts,
but actually has corresponding parallels in our
brain and nervous system.

Thus conflicts about how best to act are physical as well as mental. But a significant issue for
our time, and perhaps all times, is how we determine the actions we must take to best preserve
humanity and the environment that sustains us.
Probably even most important to consider is how
humans can work together to agree on our most
essential goals and the best path to reach them.

When things go right we often assume that
the forces of the universe are rewarding us.
When things go wrong we may assume there
is something wrong with us and we are being
punished. The reality is that our life often goes
right or wrong due to circumstances beyond our
understanding. Thinking we always control our
fate is very much a belief. This is where, once
again, a willingness to experience what comes
our way allows us to fully participate in life as

we encounter it, rather than continually judging it, which only hurts us.

We can move past our idea that we are reactive beings only capable of responding to what happens to us rather than choosing our own path. We can make choices that move us in the direction of our real goal, which is a much more loving planet for the mutual benefit of us all. Those choices become more clear as we commit ourselves to a vision of the world as a caring place. Without that commitment we will continue to feel lost. As we expand our understanding of who we are — and what we can do to improve our lives and world — we will find there is much about us to love.

Our beginning was one of connection to others and the world and of love. As we started to think of ourselves as human we began to believe that our value as individuals is dependent on what we accomplish and what others think of us. But we are much more than a set of reactions governed by others and the world around us. What happened to us in the past and what we have done cannot be changed. But the world of love we left behind can be restored. Our real self never is — and never was — the set of reactions we think it is. We are capable of identifying and working toward larger goals for ourselves and humanity — moving us back toward the world of compassion to which we all seek to return.

The following chapters explore how love is the most essential element in our efforts to work with others toward creating a society that best serves us all.

Because of you my life is now worthwhile.
– ARTHUR HAMMERSTEIN[10]

3. THE OTHER

What we know about others is what we experience in our minds. But our image never can encompass the entirety of another person.

Our usual way of knowing people is to label them, and then believe they are composed of our labels, including their gender, race, religion, age group, sexual orientation, political views, talents, social status, vocation, degree of friendliness, or any other identity we may impose on them. We put those close to us in categories like husband, wife, son, daughter, which can limit our view of them as individuals. But those labels are not who they really are. When we categorize people we often see the category rather than the person. Our ideas about others only scratch the surface of a more complex reality. We rely on the simplicity of labels to aid our understanding, but they cannot provide a complete picture of anyone.

We can begin to know others more accurately by acknowledging the limits of the veil of identity we place on them. As we set that aside we open to their ever-changing nature and extend the same recognition to them we want for ourselves. Doing this takes some humility about how little we know, and a willingness to acknowledge the unlimited essence of those with whom we interact, even though they may have limited ideas of themselves. When I remind myself I know very little about you — no matter how long I may have known you — I begin to see you more clearly.

We never can know for sure if we are connecting with the most essential part of a person. What really happens in someone's consciousness remains hidden. But we can assume there is a core in everyone — just as there is in us — that wants to be acknowledged.

We cannot define anyone by what's on the outside. We only can get to know someone by observing and interacting, which means our concept will never be static. But there is a feeling place within everyone that we can get to know by putting our concepts aside. And as we do that the feeling place within us also gets acknowledged.

Love can be experienced and expressed in

infinite ways. Although we cannot be certain what happens in anyone's mind, love expands our sense of connection. Rather than wait for others or circumstances to bring it to us, we can first allow love to ourselves and then extend it to the other person. There is no one right way to communicate other than what works to establish and maintain that connection. This makes our progress to identify and work toward mutual goals much more effective.

The emotional content behind our words conveys more than the words themselves. Love nurtures and recognizes the best in both of us at the same time. It expresses confidence in the other's value and gives that person permission to react how he or she sees fit.

When we connect only at the surface level, communication can be limited to interaction between two façades locked into positions. But we can step back and reassess whether our interaction is leading in the direction of mutual respect or creating barriers between us. We then can start to bring a genuine sense of connection into our interaction.

Because we each have different experiences in life, and thus different views of the world, I never can be sure how my efforts at communication are received. Your reaction may be different from what I expect. I only can communicate my sense of connection with another person as best I can. But I know I experience being treated well when I treat others well, and the love I express toward others affects me positively nevertheless.

The most essential part of us — the core — basically is the same. Our natural empathy — the part that connects with others — allows us to share our inner experience. Our own happiness is mirrored by the happiness we see in others. Our anger is evoked by the anger they express. Our desire for connection and recognition is reflected in the stories people tell. Words spoken by others such as happiness, sadness, joy, or trauma evoke our emotions, yet those words only capture a shadow of their impact.

My hate or judgment toward you negatively affects me, making me tense and making my breathing shallow, but it may or may not affect you at all. Even if I were to eliminate those from my life who I believe cause my negative feelings, I soon would find others to blame because the negativity in my mind awaits a chance to be projected onto someone.[11] On the other hand, as I convey appreciation to you, I experience appreciation myself. Our communication flows more easily and assumes creative forms.

When we fail to acknowledge the value of

others, they may come to believe no one cares about them, which can inspire resentment and acting out. If we want to live in a place of internal and external peace we recognize people in the same way we want to be recognized. We acknowledge the good in them and give them space to respond in their own way. There always are those who cannot be reached — at least temporarily — but there is an essential place in everyone that wants to be valued and recognized so it can spring to life.

Once we establish a sense of trust we can determine our mutual objectives and how best to work toward them. But much of our intent in communication is the emotion behind the words. We convey to others that we value them by our tone of voice as we experience being valued at the same time.

We divide others into those we believe worthy of our love and those we think are not. We create distrust in our minds when we fear that others intend us harm. When we think people may be dangerous or evil we put them into groups we consider threatening. Our discomfort may or may not be justified, but we are more likely to see others clearly by simply observing them rather than assuming the worst. When I interact respectfully with those who don't look or think like me I am more likely to get a broader perspective on the world than if I limit myself to people who already think as I do.

If we watch ourselves we can see that our reactions often are based on a threat we imagine that actually is not there. Our characterizations of others cause us to blame them for our own discomfort, or we may even want to harm them. But to fantasize harming people is different from actually inflicting it, though it may feel similar. When our emotions get the best of us we can take a deep breath and simply observe rather than reacting. This allows us to move back to the sense of connection we most want. Of course we must respond when we see that a real threat is imminent, but that is the case less often than we might assume.

Everyone longs for positive interaction. Our assumptions about people often are based on past experience with them or people we group with them. Our perception of a threat can result in distrust and conflict. There is evidence of warfare and cruelty for as long as humans have been on the earth. Skulls crushed from blows have been found in prehistoric sites. But other early sites show that some tribes lived in peace.[12] The question for us is what we can do to identify and take steps toward a world where all can live safely, working out conflicts by mutual respect rather than warfare. At this point in history we are far from that goal.

If we want to do our part to move the world — and our lives — toward greater stability and peace, we treat others with the appreciation we want for ourselves. We practice interacting in a way that reflects the kind of world in which we want to live. We open ourselves to the possibility that people are much more than our perception of them. And we can do all this while maintaining a healthy degree of caution.

Most of us have a small circle of family and friends to which we regularly extend love. We may be suspicious of those outside that realm. We have learned — by experience and the example or admonition of others — to confine our sense of connection to those who we believe worthy of our trust.

Our ideas about those we don't know change from trust to distrust along the way to becoming an adult. Our actions toward others gradually shift from openness to caution. We create degrees of separation based on how much we trust them. But our preconceptions get in the way of the relationships we really want. When we simply observe others nonjudgmentally it allows us to open new channels of communication. They may or may not meet our expectations, just as we often fail to meet our own.

Human nature is neither totally good nor bad, neither totally aggressive nor peaceful. We all have the potential for both love and hate within us.[13] When we choose to trust — or distrust — others we can base our views on evidence rather than prejudice. If evidence tells us our distrust is misplaced, it can be changed when we see that it fails to serve us.

Based on observation and experiment, many behavioral scientists are coming to the view that compassion is our most natural state.[14] When we see others suffer it causes us discomfort, although we may attempt to erect a mental wall between us and the suffering around us. But when we cut ourselves off from suffering we experience alienation. When we establish a wall we experience being walled in.

The suffering in our world seems to have no end. Poverty and homelessness negatively affect us although we try to distance ourselves. Some of us assign blame for the unfortunate state of others rather than trying to improve the situation. The horrors of war impose themselves on our minds, even from places far away, and our world rarely is without war. Our discomfort at the suffering of others is somewhat relieved when we acknowledge our connection as human beings. So the ancient question comes up for us frequently and gnaws at us in our daily lives: "Are we our brother's keeper?"

Humans always have had the potential for both aggression and peacefulness, as do many of the primates close to us. When we see violence we fear that our tendency for aggression might be provoked. But our propensity to harm others — what some would call our tendency for evil — can be turned to positive expression as we understand that our innate chronic aggression has the potential to harm us by keeping us in a state of endless anxiety. Rather, we can begin to acknowledge our common humanity in our thoughts and actions.[15]

We have an inclination toward wanting to alleviate the pain around us. But we also want to protect ourselves from the onslaught of continual suffering. Thus we often ignore the pain of others amidst the routine of our daily lives. If we were continually distracted by the suffering around us our efforts toward our own survival could be at risk. So how do we find a balance — in our minds, hearts and actions — between our own needs and moving toward the type of world in which we want to live?

There are many who — commendably

— have devoted their lives to helping people. But we've all heard the oft-repeated phrase that "charity begins in the home." Regardless of where we see ourselves along the continuum of emphasizing our own needs to helping others, love can be our guide.

What we most want — once our basic needs are met — is the experience of love. We can allow that feeling to ourselves in this moment and every moment we remember to bring it to our minds by asking ourselves: "What is love and what does it feel like?" As we confine that feeling only to some people and situations, we remove ourselves from the state we most want. Then we blame others, or the situations around us, for restricting our flow of emotion. When we limit our love that way we restrict the most essential part of who we are.

It would be naïve to assume everyone can be trusted and the entire world can be our friend. But as we begin to see that our loving nature is our essence, and our judgmental nature is less true to who we are, love becomes our guide, even while exercising caution most of the time. We remember that regardless of the façade people present, they also want to experience and express love as best they can.

For those who want a greater experience of

love in their lives — which happens to be all of us — we can allow it first with ourselves, then bring it into our interactions with others whenever and wherever possible. Circumstances will continue to put up barriers, but we can remind ourselves that our real intent is returning us and our world to a more loving place.

This never will be easy. Reality will continually pull us off track. But once again — if we choose — we can forgive others and the world for our own sake. Forgiveness moves us past our judgment and allows us to re-experience the part of us we have blocked. Rather than focusing on whether or not we can forgive, we might ask ourselves what forgiveness feels like and what we can do to move back into that state.

The quality of our lives is determined not by how much we accomplish but by how willing we are to forgive. It allows us to return to the flow of emotion we left behind. It is expressed more in how we speak than what we say. Forgiveness can be difficult. Yet still harder is holding on to judgment. Many people who have had loved ones taken from them by others seek to bring forgiveness to the responsible person for their own sake; they decide they no longer can live with a burden of hatred and blame.[16]

It's up to us whether to break the ancient

chain of human insensitivity and inhumanity or continue passing it along. We can reach out from a place deep within to that place in another that recognizes our most essential human nature and allows us to be free. When we treat people kindly we experience kindness and no longer need to await permission to feel it. As we extend love and support to others we experience love and support for ourselves.

Sometimes, after our best effort to make a relationship or friendship work, it becomes clear that it's time to move on. We can forgive a person while realizing that the connection hasn't worked and therefore is best abandoned.

There are times when we need assistance or support from others. Asking people for help — even in small ways — allows them to contribute to our need and their own self-esteem at the same time. Of course we never want to become unnecessarily dependent on others, which drags everyone down. Sometimes I ask people for assistance just to establish a connection. If people turn us down we have lost nothing. Reenforcing others' competence allows them to renew their sense of confidence.

Another concrete way we can positively affect the lives of others — and thus ourselves — is by contributing efforts and/or funds to people or organizations that improve lives. There are countless examples: volunteer in schools for students with learning issues or special needs; lend expertise to community aid organizations in areas such as accounting, law or carpentry; participate in, or make contributions to, organizations that help others build confidence and self-esteem. Although we may all be created equal, the experience of inequality is rampant in our society and in continual need of repair. Every small contribution helps while returning us to the sense of connection we seek and lifting our own self-esteem.

An important question we can ask ourselves is: Shall we continue to act automatically to others and incidents we encounter or can we move past our reactions to create the kind of world in which we want to live?

We may believe that our value as a person is determined by others or fate. When we think we look good we like ourselves. When life gives us grief our mood turns sour. Letting others — or our circumstances — determine our value means we are not convinced of our own worth. As we realize we are putting our self-respect in the hands of others we can remind ourselves of our commitment to the value of everyone, including us. This means allowing ourselves the forgiveness we seek for our shortcomings, which is a chronic issue of every human being. As we forgive ourselves we no longer depend on others for forgiveness. Our anger for their lack of understanding no longer governs us.

We may think that the judgments of others toward us — or the fate we suffer — is justified. Every day I think I could have or should have done better. There are many situations that don't work out as intended. The errors we make in a lifetime are beyond calculation. We have hurt others, embarrassed ourselves, and unintentionally made our lives more difficult than they might be. It is the human condition to act based on limited vision. At times we all regret what we have done or how things have turned out. But dwelling on remorse leaves us unable to focus on what we most want. Bringing love back to ourselves allows us to move on to engage in positive interactions with others once again.

An alternative is to deny our shortcomings and instead emphasize those of others. But this simply assigns blame for our problems and those of the world without providing a way forward. Unless we communicate and work toward common solutions our problems remain in place.

While our views of others often are based on preconceptions, our suspicions can lead to assuming the worst. We also can be influenced by those who seek political gain to exploit our distrust, which can become expressed in hateful actions that reinforce our negative views.

Some people seek simple guidelines and become mentally enslaved to leaders who tell them who is worthy and who is not. They have been convinced to be suspicious and consider themselves victims without seeing the harm of the views in which they have come to believe. They think and act based on what they are told and rarely consider whether their suspicions are true. They justify aggression by considering others less than human. They don't consider the negative consequences of their views and actions on others or society. They become henchmen for leaders who demand loyalty to themselves rather than to moral principles.

We all at our core are empathic beings. As people desert their real selves to harm others, their conscience gnaws at them. It seeks to return them to a belief in the value of people so they can at the same time value themselves. We can — as caring individuals and citizens concerned about the state of our world — remind others about how they are hurting themselves as they back the false view that some people are less human than others. They may not be aware that they seek an ideal world free from those they think burden it, but we can point out that the world they really want only can be brought about by devotion to the principle of valuing all human beings. Of course we would communicate that message in our own words, hopefully in a compassionate way that can be heard.

Whatever our actions, or whatever others may think or say of us, or whatever fate we may suffer, our essence remains the same. What changes is our self-image based on how we or others view us. It only seems that our true nature is subject to forces outside of us because that is what we have come to believe.

Our vision is limited to the little we can see, rather than the vastness of the real world, and we usually act based on that limited view. Our decisions don't always turn out to have been the wisest choices once we see the larger picture. Although we may learn from experience, it always is too late to change the past. And our repeated automatic reactions to others make us wonder at times if learning really is possible. Based on our history, our reactive self is unlikely to go away. So we continually wonder if there is a way out.[17]

This is where love comes in, which only is one word for our most basic human state. We consistently lose contact with that part of us. But as we learn to bring greater forgiveness and awareness to ourselves, despite missteps due to our limited vision, we are governed by our reactive self less often and more often bring light and awareness to our actions. We see the larger picture, that is we can bring love directly into our lives. And when we forget and once again act based on our limited vision, we can forgive ourselves as we hopefully learn and move on.

Reclaiming the most essential part of us brings us back to our natural sense of wonder and well-being. It is the key to our reconnection with others. We experience the love within us as we acknowledge it with or without permission of others.

Regardless of what we pretend, we are connected to the suffering of others, which we experience in our minds and the discomfort of our bodies. Others' suffering is our suffering and the only way to ease that is compassion. When we give love, we get love. We experience being treated well as we treat others well, and hope that view can be spread to a world very much in need of it.

*"A community is a group of people
with a common project."*
– DAVID BROOKS[18]

4. THE GROUP

Dialogue between two people allows them to identify and work toward common goals. In groups of three or more the dynamic changes. An intentional entity is created with rules — formal or informal — about how interactions between members are to take place. The intent of the group can be friendship, enhancing survival, or combining forces to benefit its members and possibly others.

Groups are common in the natural world. They are found from the level of the most primitive organisms to human beings. Cells combine to create simple life forms and also to enable the existence of complex plants and animals. Group behavior of ants, flight patterns of bird flocks, as well as hunting practices of primates and humans are crucial for their survival.

Joining groups is essential for our success. We choose our group affiliations based on a common purpose or like minds. We adopt group identities that become part of how we think of ourselves, such as religion, ethnicity, gender, race or political affiliation.[19] We give our groups many names such as family, tribe, band or organization, but their essential purpose is the same: they enable us to combine efforts toward a common cause.

Individuals and families always have formed groups. Early tribes were egalitarian; decisions were made among members for how to hunt, where to live, and how to treat each other.[20] As tribes grew larger, rules were made by leaders at a greater distance from those they governed. These included behavioral guidelines that were conveyed verbally and eventually written down. But rules and laws — though necessary — can be seen by some to curtail spontaneity as well as individual expression and choice, which encourages them to consider themselves above the law or to rebel against authority. Rebellions have been recorded in societies throughout history.

In small groups, a supportive connection exists among people who know each other, which means that rules can be simple and flexible. Larger groups require rules or laws that continually can be revised as they anticipate a larger range of behaviors. They only can be changed by leaders or, in democracies, consensus of members or their representatives. As groups grow, their rules — and then laws — become more complex. For one example, the founding of the United States was rooted in small colonies with their own governance that eventually joined forces and forged more comprehensive laws.

As groups grew, production of food and goods such as clothing became more specialized. Evidence from prehistoric times shows that many traded with each other to obtain items they didn't produce themselves, such as pottery or jewelry.[21] The advent of a shared language also strengthened group identity.

The development of agriculture, about 11,000 years ago, allowed groups to settle in one place. Leaders needed to create more comprehensive laws as towns, and then cities, grew larger. In some, such as Athens with its democracy, lawmaking was assigned to a subgroup of citizens.

Groups become more stable when they fulfill a clear purpose that benefits their members, such as increased prosperity or greater freedom. Individuals in stable groups experience a connection with other members that positively affects their lives and interactions. A sense of shared purpose also can be based on honoring a group's ethnicity, race, or beliefs. Our affinity for those we see as like us or having common interests causes us to favor them in our minds and actions. Those outside our group may be viewed suspiciously and not afforded the same amount of trust.

A sense of common purpose allows us to extend our feeling of connection to people we don't even know. Groups are more likely to thrive when personal support and recognition are an essential part of how they function. Effective leadership keeps them on track by reminding them of their purpose. In well-functioning groups, members look out for the interest of others. Supportive connections are part of the makeup of animal groups as well as those of people. For example, rhesus monkeys scream to warn each other of danger.[22]

Some groups, such as charitable organizations, have a purpose of helping those less fortunate. They range from small efforts with just a few volunteers to large multi-billion dollar global non-government organizations (NGOs) formed to reduce poverty and disease.

Groups develop shared values about how members should act, which include behavioral codes. But they often engage in judgments about those outside their group based on a stated or unstated belief in their superiority.

A group's values permeate the minds of its members. Values can include honesty, compassion, loyalty, generosity, fairness, reliability and respect toward each other. Some groups — particularly in democracies — stand for upholding the dignity and rights of all people.

But some advocate for the advantage of their members at the expense of others. This limits their sense of connection to only those who look or think like them. That perspective can impart a belief to members of being cut off from those outside the group, or even from the rest of humanity, which leads to a sense of isolation. Members of such groups may consider themselves persecuted even though they may not be part of a minority, such as is the case with white supremacists.[23]

We seek certainty in a world that seems full of uncertainty. Many people are attracted to groups with leaders and views that provide that certainty for them. Adopting group values and beliefs can allow people to think they know what is true — or that they are right — and confirms their validity as human beings. People also want to know they have a purpose in life, which may include working with group members toward common goals. This may be seen in those who join political parties.

When rigid views about others are shared among group members it provides a sense of comfort and certainty. For some groups the purpose is eliminating threats from others that are real or imagined. Members may become willing to believe "truths" told them by leaders rather than making their own observations and coming to conclusions based on evidence. Those beliefs can include that members of other groups are inferior, or not quite human, or that they are a threat.

A charismatic leader can become the focus of love and worship by group members, whether or not that person serves their best interests. Members can fail to consider if their leader continues to champion the principle of making their lives or the world better that inspired their involvement in the first place. As a group moves toward authoritarianism, supporters no longer question what they are told. Devotion to a political party or leader can deceive people into thinking they are voting for their own good while they actually support an autocrat posed to take away their freedoms. Within this century we have seen this happen in Russia, Hungary, and a number of other nations. George Washington famously warned about loyalty to a political party, rather than staying focused on principles, in his *Farewell Address.*[24]

In extreme cases a group's purpose can become to persecute, or even exterminate, other groups. At first the intent of the Nazi party in the 1930s was to marginalize what they considered inferior groups, which is the goal of extremist organizations in many countries in our own day. The danger of their views became clear when they gained power and began persecuting those they marginalized. Eliminating conquered groups even was common in societies that our "advanced" civilization considers primitive, as revealed by archeological evidence. Some dominant tribes practiced slavery, human sacrifice and even defilement of the skulls of other groups.[25] Ancient Greeks enslaved many of their conquered enemies they didn't kill.[26]

Just as we once sought assurance and love from our parents, leaders who exude certainty convince us that they know what is true. They provide an experience of being listened to and loved. Since love is the ambrosia we want above all else, we are reluctant to give it up. Even if we become concerned about the behavior or hateful message of charismatic leaders, we are likely to put that aside and stay with them for the emotional reward they provide. We become oblivious to views different than those expressed by our leader. And since we think we now know the truth, we see our group and its beliefs as superior. We dismiss our own ideas of right and wrong to follow our leader rather than submitting to the "evil" world that we have become convinced threatens us.

But our certainty comes at a cost. It creates a filter through which we see the world and blinds us to much of reality outside of what we already believe. It chokes off our intelligence and capacity to love. It erects a barrier between us and those we consider different from ourselves. The filters through which we see the world echo to us what we already believe. Psychologists call this confirmation bias.[27]

Our group instinct can serve or harm us. An advantage of groups is their scale; they provide coordinated efforts to protect us and serve our needs. A disadvantage can be the belief that only we and our group members are valid human beings, and that to survive we must marginalize others or eliminate them altogether. This view has led to conflicts throughout human history; to costly wars and genocide. The result often has been the decimation of one side with the loss of many lives on both sides. It also brings the perennial fear of believing there always is an enemy out there that threatens us with another war in which we may be the next to be destroyed.

Blind cult behavior leads to undermining the value of making the world better that originally attracted people to the group. As an autocratic leader gains power, even supporters no longer are safe. When they realize their own rights are threatened, it may be too late to change the leader's grip on power. This has been the result of many movements in history, including revolutions in France, Russia and China.

Elevating oneself and one's group above others only accomplishes a temporary advantage that will again need to be defended when the next enemy is identified. The vision and hope for greatness becomes absorbed in hateful rhetoric. When the focus always is on what a group is against rather than what it is for, enmity and internal strife never end. Group members lose their way as adherence to absolute authority replaces their hope for making the world better. George Orwell's novel *1984*, written soon after World War II, features a society that is kept focused on an ever-changing enemy and provides us a warning of this exact possibility.

Chronic enmity and war afflicts members of groups that are in conflict or have the potential for conflict, which includes all of us. But we can choose to return to a view more in touch with our compassionate nature regardless of the views common in our society. We can acknowledge our common humanity with those within our group and without. We can open channels of communication to work with others toward a vision that best serves us all despite our differences. We can realize that our group is one of many struggling to make the world better; that understanding can restore the experience of connection we once had. When we judge others we hurt ourselves which may or may not affect the people we judge. But when we acknowledge the value of others we experience being valued.

Our behavior often is a reaction to others and events, just like the pre-humans from which we evolved and much of the animal kingdom. It may seem we have no control over our actions. The difference is that humans are self-aware. We can establish a sense of common purpose, working with others in dialogue toward an inclusive vision.

This provides an opportunity to discuss consciousness — the part of each of us that observes the rest. It seems to me likely that consciousness evolved slowly as species gradually became more aware of themselves. As mentioned, some animals are conscious of impending danger and even warn others of it. This means they have an idea about themselves and concern about others like them. So there is a degree of self-awareness and empathy among some other species. At the level of humans we become conscious of being separate individuals who want to perpetuate ourselves at least for the span of a lifetime.[28]

As infants we saw others and the world without judgment, and it is to that view we long to return. This becomes clear as we observe young children who interact openly and model nonjudgmental behavior. As we join forces with others to form groups, which is part of our success as a species, our tribal instinct to defend ourselves and our group can take over. Our competitiveness can turn to treachery. We establish comradery within our own group but can refuse to extend it to the "other" — members of groups to which we consider ourselves superior or we think endanger us. We can decline to expand our natural democratic instinct — the part of us that trusts and works together with others — beyond our group because of our fear of the aggression we have witnessed and also carry in our genes.

Every expression of hate toward others based on their group has the potential to blossom into violence. Holding hatred in our hearts and minds — and then expressing it — can lead to harm to others and ourselves. The alternative is first acknowledging that place of love and compassion within us and then bringing the understanding we want for ourselves to others. This is how we progress toward creating the world in which we want to live.

We can choose to learn not only from history, but from the devastation of the enmity and wars all around us in our own day where nobody wins. Limiting our connection to only our own group or those who think like us can lead to our own decimation. If we want to ensure our survival and that of our group, our only real choice is to extend our group identity to all of humanity. That moves us in the direction of our real goal, which is being secure in our connection with others.

Rather than casting suspicion and disdain on people because of the groups to which they belong, we can support them as they celebrate their heritage and identity, except for celebrations based on an idea of superiority. Others may also want to support us in commemorating our significant events. This moves us toward a world where the ethnicity and beliefs of all are valued. In an atmosphere where we are free to honor our culture, others are free to honor theirs. To respect the diversity of others is to respect the diverse aspects of ourselves.

Of course there is nothing wrong with competition between groups. Games are an ancient tradition that allow us to participate in activities to gain skills and honor the talents of participants rather than threatening harm. The original Olympics in Greece brought together competitors from cities all over their part of the world.

We all have the potential for two basic views within us: (1) all are equally valid human beings deserving of respect and dignity, or (2) one group (ours) is superior to others. If you think that no one is born inferior to anyone else, you are on the side of democracy. If you believe in your own superiority or that of your group, or those who think or look like you, you are on the side of authoritarianism.

Our sense of validity as human beings comes from recognizing and opening ourselves to the essential loving being we really are. It doesn't come from others or our group. In this moment — and every moment — we can remind ourselves about our true purpose: returning to an experience of love and bringing that feeling to ourselves, which we then can extend to those within our group and without.

We can move beyond our reactive selves to engage others based on our higher selves, the part that recognizes the value of every human being and acts on that knowledge. As we choose to open ourselves to what we most want — the experience of connection with others — we confirm that we are the masters of our own fate.

5. THE NATION

Animals and humans enhance their chances of survival by joining families and groups, but only humans can conceive and create a nation. Only we can prioritize allegiance to our nation over love of ourselves or group. One result of the advent of nations is their stability. Other results have been unfettered patriotism and destructive wars on a scale that otherwise would not be possible.

In the minds of many people, the terms nation and country are virtually the same. For our purposes we will use both terms interchangeably.[30] But there are some differences to consider. A nation is a large cohesive group with a history of common identity. Nations — or national alliances — can operate separately from borders. A nation can be an ethnic group like the Jews or "Nation of Islam" claim to be. It also can be the identity of a people such as the German state.

A country is a legal entity with clear territory and borders. Countries result from the expansion of groups and the domination of one over others, usually as a result of war. Many countries — unlike groups with a natural affinity — are held together by artificial means. Our membership in countries expands our sense of connection to people with whom we otherwise may have no common bond. The borders of countries are stable at any one time but can be changed. Poland, for example, has had different borders as a result of invading forces. After a 1795 partition among three nations, Poland disappeared from the map, and since has reappeared in various forms. But many would claim there is a long-standing Polish identity.

Most nations have their origins in groups that have existed for centuries. But our modern nations were forged relatively recently in human history. Those that have existed in the same form as in our day go back only about 200 years. Although there were many periods of peace and stability, history records many wars of independence between regions and nations that want to bring them into their fold. This continues into our day as Russia tries to reconquer Ukraine and Israel seeks to expand into Palestinian territory. Some people in areas of Europe and elsewhere still consider their primary loyalty to their group, such as in the Catalan region of Spain and the Kurdistan region of Iraq. The only current stable government that goes back much over 200 years is that of San Marino, population 35,000, at the northern tip of Italy, with a constitution written in 1600.

Groups migrated out of Africa about 70,000 years ago into what is now Europe and Asia. The oldest Middle Eastern civilization dates to about 3500 BCE in present-day Iraq. What now is a united Greece first was settled in about 3000 BCE by the Mycenean civilization on the island of Cyprus, eventually leading to the dominance of Athens and other Greek city-states over much of the ancient world. Rome, also a city-state, was founded about 600 BCE, and ruled much of what is now Europe as far north as present-day England until about 400 AD. Charlemagne created the Holy Roman Empire under the Catholic Church, beginning in the year 800, that eventually became what we now know as Germany, Austria, Belgium, the Netherlands, Switzerland, plus parts of France, Denmark, Poland, and Italy. The United Kingdom of Britain and Ireland came into existence in 1801, and only became a democracy with the passage of the First Reform Act of 1832 which extended the vote to seven percent of men. The right to vote was not extended to men and women over 18 until 1969.

In Asia, China had over 100 dynasties ruling all or parts of its territory from about 2000 BCE to its 1911 revolution, with its current Communist regime gaining power in 1949. Historians divide Japanese history into fourteen periods, from its hunter-gatherer origins over 2000 years ago to the present. It's current government and constitution were founded after its loss in World War II.

In Africa, small kingships of Egypt that go back 6000 years eventually merged into two that were united in 3100 BCE. Egypt had a series of dynasties until overthrown by the Persians in 343 BCE, that soon after was conquered by the Greeks, followed by the Romans in 30 BCE. Muslim rule started in 641. The British dominated from the 1800s until forced out in 1954. The Republic of Egypt was run by Gamal Abdel Nasser until his death in 1970, then a series of coups led to the current government which only has been in place since 2013. The rest of Africa has 54 countries often subject to coups, but only a handful of stable governments with varying degrees of democracy have been founded over the last 60 years.[31] These include Mauritius, Botswana, Cape Verde, Namibia, Ghana, and South Africa, that adopted a new constitution after the end of apartheid in 1994.

In the Western Hemisphere, European colonists decimated populations — some advanced — that had been in existence for 5000 years. Spain ruled most of South and Central America beginning about 1500, except for Brazil which was under Portugal, and both were ousted by revolutions after 300 years. North America was colonized first by Spain, then England, and soon after by the Dutch and French, but these territories expelled their colonial powers as they expanded and gained strength. The United States, founded in 1776, is the oldest country with a consistent stable democratic government. Canada only gained independence from Great Britain in 1867.

The conflicts between what would become nations began as disputes between kings to determine who would hold the crown. Famous among these is the Battle of Agincourt of 1415, made legendary by Shakespeare in his play *Henry V*, in which Henry inspires his "band of brothers" to victory over a larger French force. But England and France were not the centralized nations they would become. Toward the end of the Middle Ages, what we now know as France still was in the throes of conflicting principalities, and England was in a struggle to determine who would rule. This also was the case in much of Europe, with Italy not being united until 1871, and the unification of Germany coming in the same year. Germany was divided into East and West after World War II and only reunited in 1990.

The development of nations is a challenge even for historians to track. Nevertheless nations have resulted in both great benefits and great devastation to humanity. Their stability has allowed — particularly in democracies — multiple innovations that have advanced their standard of living and that of much of the world.

Considering the mass destruction foisted upon our world by conflicts between nations, we might ask ourselves where our allegiance should be. Most people profess loyalty to their nation as a priority over their groups, or even over their families and selves. The number of people killed in wars between groups pales in comparison with those lost in conflicts between nations that also have decimated large civilian populations. Wars of this scale have taken place from those of Napoleon, that began in 1803, to World War II.

The great onslaughts of nations against each other began as they solidified into large blocks whose leaders were able to command armies of a size not previously known: over 2 million men for Napoleon, twice the size of the previous largest army of 1 million of the 15th century Ming Dynasty, and 3 million for the German army of World War I. And the larger the army the greater the slaughter.

So we might ask ourselves: "What is it that motivates us to build gradually larger armies that are able to kill greater numbers of people?" and "What is it in our makeup that allows us to participate in escalating slaughter?"

In our minds — which tend to be polarized — we readily paint people, groups and nations as good or evil. Once we determine what we believe is their nature, we are reluctant to remove them from those categories.[32] We want to believe we are right and sound in our judgment, and also want to know who to trust, so we rarely look beyond the elevation or condemnation we project onto other nations. In the meantime they place us in the same categories.

Our views of nations — and their people — often are over-simplified and misleading, rather than based on thoughtful evaluation. We — and our governments — often create profiles that lack depth, yet they shape our actions. Russia once was good, then evil, then good, now evil again. Vietnam, in our view, was riddled with Communists that threatened our existence, thus we lost 58,000 soldiers there. But now that country is a major trading partner.

All countries are made up of people not much different from ourselves. Yet placing them into categories of good and evil can lead to war and the slaughter of thousands of innocents. To prevent devastation on a mass scale, is it possible to move past our automatic judgments and see other people, groups and nations more accurately? And if so, how would we do that?

Humans have evolved to come to quick conclusions about who and what is good or bad, safe or dangerous, which has been a significant factor in our success. But that also makes us more likely to engage in conflict or go to war. We could make more accurate decisions if we were to consider the factors that go into them more carefully. Daniel Kahneman has researched our decision-making process and summarized his findings in his widely read book *Thinking Fast and Slow*. He states that we have the capacity for both reactive thought and an ability to make well-considered decisions.[33]

We often operate more on our gut reaction than constructing a balanced picture of people and nations. Our destructive 2003 attack on Iraq based on misinformation is an example. The process we often use can provide a convenient shortcut for decision-making, but also can lead to mistakes and regret. Our decisions may be based on anger, an immediate reaction to what we see as danger, or a feeling of suspicion that may or may not be based on evidence. When we take the time to allow ourselves to come to a balanced view, the outcome is likely to be more realistic.

Love of our nation doesn't mean it always is right. We can evaluate whether our leaders are pursuing a wise or necessary course and provide feedback when we think they make ill-considered decisions. We may be likely to rally behind poor policy when told there is a threat, but that often is the trick of leaders who want to justify decisions they already have made.

People and situations are more complex than our ideas about them. It is common to make automatic judgments rather than holding off on conclusions until we have more complete information. This even can happen when we characterize an entire nation. Snap judgments are easier to make than considering a more balanced view. In the same way, most of us have changed our ideas about some people once we have gotten to know them.

Somewhere within us we know there is more to people — and their nations — than the characterizations we thrust upon them. We know this because we are aware of our own complexity. We want recognition as does everyone, including the inhabitants of other nations. As we get to know people and nations we begin to see them as very much like ourselves. We realize there is more to them than we had assumed.

The only way to get to know people is by taking time to interact. The same applies to relationships between nations. What we think about others always is based on limited information, which is why travel is so enlightening. Nations — like people — are composed of countless aspects that make up their totality. If our leaders truly listen to each other they can see that there is fear and insecurity on the other side as well as on our own. Building positive connections includes working together toward trust that could result in trade that benefits both sides. But trade agreements between nations need to include consideration of the conditions of everyone affected, including workers, otherwise what appears as a benefit to a nation can be to the detriment of those who dwell there.

Another important question we can ask is: "Should our loyalties primarily be to ourselves, our groups or our nations?" We also might consider if we really have a choice. If drafted into

an army, for example, our nation will take prece-
dence in our lives if not in our minds.

Every nation is composed of unique individuals essentially like us. But we often are taught
to emphasize our differences and we easily can
assume that our uniqueness makes us better
than others. A degree of pride can bring out the
best in us. But if we dwell on our differences
rather than what we have in common and the
value of cooperation, the ultimate result can be
devastating for both sides.

Within nations there always has been a
divide between the interests of the elite — people who control societies — and those of the
average person. In early Athens, about 600 BCE,
a leader name Solon tried to limit the dominance
of wealthy lenders that kept the average person subjugated and was exiled for his efforts.
About 200 years later, Socrates taught followers
the importance of cultivating wisdom to guide
one's actions rather than automatically comply-
ing with what they were told. He was executed
for his efforts. And so it goes throughout history. There have been countless individuals
and groups that have — publicly or privately
— followed their conscience rather than sub-
mit to what leaders expect. This often has led
to persecution, and at times to revolution. But

revolutionary leaders also can form a new elite, which results in renewed resistance.

The idea of democracy — a word that means rule or government by the people in the ancient Greek language — is an impulse that goes to the heart of every human being. It comes from the time when our input was valued as we lived in small groups.[34] We all know that the best government recognizes and serves our needs. The success of modern democracy depends on a population that insists leaders consider what is best for the greatest number of people and are working together to implement that model. Maintaining democracy takes dedication and collaboration toward a path that best serves all — a path that needs to be constantly updated. This is a challenge considering how many interests and views must be taken into account. But the alternative is giving over governance to leaders and hoping for the best, which history has shown rarely works out.

Most people under democratic governments take their freedoms for granted and hand over their decision-making process to leaders or parties instead of developing their own ideas of what makes their country work. But those in power often are more motivated to staying there than to maintaining a democratic government.

So people who want to preserve their democracy must remain involved, at least at some level.

There are two kinds of love that can bind us to our nation: love of our country, which includes all of its citizens, or love of a leader. Love of a leader easily can result in an autocracy that people regret. Leaders who are not committed to democracy often try to stay in power by identifying an enemy — internal or external — that the majority can hate rather than moving toward a more responsive government. Examples in our own time can be seen in India and Hungary, once exemplary democratic nations, where leaders maintain authority by evoking the prejudices of the majority against minorities. Many people are willing to be convinced by their leaders that they are better than others, which moves them toward internal conflict or confrontation with other nations.

This brings us to the topic of nationalism.

Nationalism, according to the Oxford Dictionary, is *identification with one's own nation and support for its interests, especially to the exclusion or detriment of the interests of other nations.*

According to political scientist Walker Connor:

The essence of a nation... is a psychological bond that joins a people and differentiates it in the subconscious conviction of its members from all other people in a most vital way.[35]

A psychological bond involves the level of feeling as well as that of thought.

Other scholars maintain that a nation is based on a common belief in it among its members. Social anthropologist Ernest Gellner tells us:

Nations as a natural, God-given way of classifying men, as an inherent though long-delayed political destiny, are a myth.[36]

Geller is telling us that nations are not necessarily natural entities. He goes on with his view of nationalism:

Nationalism...sometimes takes pre-existing cultures and turns them into nations, sometimes invents them, and often obliterates pre-existing cultures.

According to this view a nation can be as much a created entity as a natural one.

Nations may have their basis in history or have a more recent identity forged by strong leaders. Because of our natural desire to be part of a group, pride in our nations probably goes back to when they first appeared. Expanding our love of our group to that of our nation allows us to establish a common bond while providing greater safety for inhabitants and honoring their diversity and skills.

Since almost no one considers their nation

interior to others, there is an element of pride in our national identity that benefits us when we engage or trade with other nations, but leads to grief when our competition turns to war.

To love our country doesn't mean we only love those who look and act like us or meet our approval. It means we honor every individual of which it is made, including those we think of as good and bad, beautiful and ugly, people of all colors and hues. It means we respect the dignity of everyone who makes up the fabric of our nation.

Avoiding destructive diplomatic relations lies in the ability of leaders to look beyond the façade of other nations, just like in successful human relations.[37] What works best is recognizing the value and uniqueness of those nations with which we interact and their people. Different nations represent different cultures, and when our own culture promotes tolerance and support for each individual, our leaders will be more likely to engage in interactions that emphasize common understanding rather than differences.

We can evoke a sense of connection to those with whom we interact and to every member of our group. We then can expand that to all those who constitute our nation.

Being human, we will forget what works best and find ourselves honoring only parts of our nation while feeling contempt for others. Then — if we really love our country — we can put our effort into respecting the dignity of everyone, which will be an ongoing challenge because of our habit of dividing all we encounter into categories of good and bad. When our energy is spent on building up our nations — and those who inhabit them — rather than tearing them down, we bring to ourselves the feeling of love we seek.

"Humans only have one ending;
ideas live forever."
– FROM THE MOVIE BARBIE, 2023[38]

6. THE WORLD

We are genetically linked with all of humanity from birth.[39] Our membership in a nation or citizenship in a country may change. We even may be a "person without a country." But we always have been — and always will be — fellow citizens of the world.

From our very beginning we feel connected to everything and everyone, then eventually begin to think of ourselves as members of a family, group or nation. Our divisions guide us but also lead us astray. They sharpen our focus but keep us from fully experiencing and appreciating the people and world around us.

We are born to a world of wholeness — of oneness — and slowly change to a view of a world divided into what we think of as good and evil, right and wrong, light and dark, who or what we should love or hate. Polarizing the world this way keeps us from actually seeing it. When we judge people and the world we experience judgment, and when we feel hate we experience it in our minds and bodies.[40] We long to return to our original sense of connectedness throughout our lives.[41]

The world itself remains whole and oblivious to our thoughts and judgments. When we move past the divisions and preconceptions in our minds we have a clearer view; we allow ourselves to experience the world in its wholeness once again. We then can choose to honor that vision in our words and actions.

The world will tell us its story if we watch closely, which can serve as a guide for our interactions with it and its inhabitants. The story we most often see is of the earth being torn apart and reconnecting to itself; extreme violence alternating with peacefulness. But that view is a reflection of our own fluctuations of perception and mood. The world itself doesn't know of these fluctuations; there is nothing in its mind. It expresses itself in an ongoing thrust regardless of our perceptions. It belches and grunts and moans and rests in an continuous expression of the chaos in which it was conceived. And we who dwell there only can do our best to cope.

We all have ideas for how we want the world

to be, and often are disillusioned. We hope for it to be our mother; a calm and supportive presence from which we can milk kindness and nurturance. But the world goes about being itself, never cognizant of our efforts to tame it. We do our best to adjust to its unpredictable nature as it functions by its own rules and not ours. When we really pay attention we begin to understand that it never will comply with our ideas of how it should be, and we resign ourselves to the possibility that our understanding and descriptions always will fall short because the world truly is beyond our comprehension.[42]

We never will experience the fulfillment from our world for which we hope, where all goes as planned and people look and act as we expect. But if willing to recognize that we set ourselves up for disappointment by holding unreasonable expectations, we can put those aside as we acknowledge the unpredictable nature of people and reality.

The infinitely varied humans who share our world — both those close to us and at a distance — never will meet our ideals of how they should be. We only can learn more about people as best we can and appreciate them as they are, including their lack of predictability. This can lead to more harmonious interactions. We then can more easily set shared goals to improve all of our lives.

But then starts the hard part. Despite similar words we may use to describe our visions for the type of world we want, the actual visions we hold in our minds will vary. I may use the word "freedom," for example, and you may seem to agree, but what we each mean by "freedom" is likely to differ. Some may consider freedom to be important for themselves and their group; others may believe that real freedom applies to everyone. Making freedom a lived reality for people by agreements, rules or laws takes lengthy and patient negotiation. And then maintaining it requires continual monitoring. Committed communication by individuals, groups and nations is needed in the pursuit of our vision of a world that works for all. But that process often is marred by individuals or nations that attempt to impose their views on others rather than working toward a consensus.

The idea of the proper function of government many people hold in their minds is to guarantee freedom for themselves and those they think of as like them, but often not for groups or nations they see as unlike them or undeserving. Leaving the interests of some people out inevitably leads to resentment, and often rebellion, as happened at the founding of the

United States and in countless countries since. The US *Declaration of Independence,* composed after its 1776 rebellion, and France's *Declaration of the Rights of Man and Citizen,* written in the wake of its 1789 revolution, set ideals for the equal treatment of every human being that still have not been fully realized. Guaranteeing those rights requires continual dialogue to overcome the barriers in the way of recognizing the validity of others as equal to ourselves.

To move past communication barriers within — and among — nations requires patience and commitment, particularly in the presence of powerful individuals and countries who seek to control the agenda. People want to know that those who claim to serve them have their best interests in mind. But this requires citizen involvement in monitoring the efforts of their leaders.

Robert Keohane, who has written many books on international relations, tells us:

Americans... could try to understand more about world politics, to become both less arrogant toward other cultures and political systems, and more resolved to play a positive role in improving the often horrible conditions of life that contribute to support for terrorism and other types of violence...Such an orientation will require more openness toward information...even, or especially, information that makes us uncomfortable, such as information about the negative views of American policy held by many people in the world.[43]

If we watch ourselves in the course of our daily lives, we can see that our thoughts toward others vary from peacefulness to fear and aggression, sometimes even with no instigation from the other person. We blame others for invoking the aggressive thoughts that are part of our nature.[44] The human tendency to condemn others for our own discomfort can result in conflict that is played out on a national or even international scale. But when we acknowledge our aggressive side, we can forgive and move past that part of us as we work to establish the peaceful interactions we really want.

If we desire a more caring world for ourselves, we can begin by moving in that direction in everyday interactions despite our human limitations. By acknowledging the essence of people — which is much like our own — we can bring them the recognition they seek and experience it at the same time. We can show appreciation for others — and their nations — despite their behaviors based on what they may believe about us. Ultimately, for everyone, the experience of peace is the goal we hold in the back of our minds.

We have seen peace come to nations that were thought by many to be engaged in intractable conflict. Apartheid ended in South Africa with agreement to share governance among previous combatants, as did the long and destructive wars of Northern Ireland. These agreements were among people who had a long history of enmity and violence, but they decided to move beyond the past to create a new present that benefits them all. Even now, the old enmity flares up at times in these places, and they struggle to remind themselves that an uneasy peace is vastly preferable to the destructive behaviors of the past.

There is no "real" or objective character of people, nations or even the world that the human mind can comprehend. When we see our lives as fulfilling we find the world friendly and supportive; when we see our lives as disappointing we seek someone or something to blame. To aid our understanding, we developed tools such as science, philosophy, religion, literature, and art. But when we allow our emotions — or those who evoke them — to take control of our minds we displace understanding with a return to the aggressiveness we thought we had left behind.

One only need look at how the Germany of World War II was transformed from a country that had in many ways been at the height of human accomplishment to see how we need to be on guard against the part of us that seeks to harm people rather than honor them.

Aggression is built into us because it once had survival value, particularly in tribal warfare.[45] But cooperation is much more in keeping with survival in our own time.[46] If we choose, we can move past our ingrained negative views of other groups and nations that lead to aggression as we acknowledge the limits of our understanding. We can open ourselves to the discovery of the real nature of others. It takes humility to let go of views that may be long held, but a deeper understanding has the potential to alter our insights and actions as we attempt to move toward the world we envision. When we look beyond our preconceptions we find that others — at their core — are much like us. This may lead to expanding our identification from just our own group or nation to all of humanity. When we see the world as harsh and hostile, we experience our lives as harsh and hostile; when we see the peaceful side of our world and its inhabitants we experience the peace we seek.

Thus the world we see is a reflection of what

is inside us. Movement toward the peaceful world we imagine must involve insight into the defensive nature of our minds. Acknowledging this allows us to begin to progress beyond it.

We each hold within us an ideal of a vision where the world will be as we want it to be and others will act as we want them to act. This is reflected in every religion and philosophy. But if you look back at your own history, whether it spans five or ninety-five years, you might notice that rarely have you thought things are fine as they are. We think if only others or the world would meet our hopes and expectations that we will be happy at last. Thus it is for the entire human race. We might look realistically at the times for which we now long to return because we think things went well — otherwise known as nostalgia. But at those times we also were hoping for things to get better. The ideal world we imagine always has been — and always will be — out of reach because we perpetually place it in the future.

The present rarely is good enough in our minds. Thus we all are inadvertent utopians imagining a time when the world will at last meet our expectations. But if that ever were to happen, it clearly is human nature to move the goal posts to deprive ourselves of appreciating where we are in any moment. When we arrive in heaven it will take us little time to begin focusing on its faults.

So we might ask ourselves: do we want to spend our lives in discontent, or would we prefer to clarify our vision of how we want the world to be — together with the other imperfect human beings who inhabit our planet — and do all we can to move toward that? As mentioned, a problem we will encounter is that the words we use, such as peace or happiness, will invoke a different image for different people. Thus our only choice — if we really care to move toward the world we envision — is to engage in dialogue at the level of the individual, group, nation and world, and to commit ourselves to continue on the path of working toward that vision, which may be an ongoing process for the rest of our lives and as long as we inhabit the planet. We may never accomplish our ideal, but taking steps toward it is its own reward. Perhaps we all can agree that is preferable to war.

The degree of physical comfort in which most people live has vastly improved over the last 100 years, including health outcomes and life expectancy, at least in the Western world. But amidst our progress we have overheated the planet and created a pollution nightmare that endangers our existence. Our earth and oceans are heating at a steady pace that contributes to unprecedented wildfires and storms that have become more frequent. We always seem to be on the verge of committing ourselves to eliminating the toxins that have accumulated in our environment and threaten our health and that of our planet, but our progress has been too slow to reliably mitigate the problem. The large industrial nations have contributed the most toward what could become an environmental disaster. It is their responsibility to lead the rest of the world in avoiding it by taking bold and specific steps toward reversing what has become a global crisis.[47]

Most of us are concerned about the suffering we see due to poverty, war, illness, cruelty, and other misfortune. We want to do what we can to alleviate it or, perhaps for some of us, avoid it altogether. But all we know about suffering is what we experience. So to the extent we alleviate suffering we reduce our own. As young children we were empathic to the discomfort we saw, then slowly erected a wall that allowed us to focus on our everyday tasks. Relieving the suffering around us begins with allowing ourselves to return to the connection to people we once felt and now experience only as concepts as we refuse to allow others into our minds and hearts. As we do that we deprive ourselves of the connections to which we want to return. That includes the experience of joy, anger, and other emotions we deny to ourselves.

The real world is not the one of our perceptions. It's not a collection of people and houses and cars and other things. It's a continuous series of everchanging events that we can better understand by allowing ourselves to experience it. This happens in a way that words cannot adequately capture. We can allow the joy and sorrow that pulses through the world to also go through us. As we do this we become more attuned to all that surrounds us.

We have a tradition of cruelty toward others that predates history. Evidence is continually being found of the horrors that humans have inflicted on each other from the earliest of times. Scientists now believe that tribes not only tortured others as they defeated them, but tore apart and desecrated their bodies, perhaps to cement their sense of superiority. Anthropologists have found evidence among Southwest native Americans of the sacrifice of the defeated, and even cannibalism.[48] Over 2000 years ago Scythians turned the skin of their enemies into pouches.[49]

When we seek vengeance toward other

nations — and their inhabitants — it adds to our own suffering. Assigning blame to others never ends because it doesn't bring us relief. Its results can be disastrous for both sides. One example: the victors of World War I tried to levy reparations on Germany that could not reasonably be paid. The result was seething resentment that led to World War II, a much more deadly conflict.

The alternative is seeing the interests of others as our own. When we do what we can to alleviate their suffering we contribute to our own relief. That even works when we empathize with their anger. When we see and honor the value of others, we experience our own value. The victors of World War II did learn from the results of their previous punitive actions and helped to rebuild Germany and Japan, which today are bastions of democracy and among our most crucial allies.

Peace is not just the absence of war. It is an experience both within and without ourselves. As long as we have an enemy in our minds we will be at war with someone — mentally or physically — and we will experience the anxiety brought by our blame. Our perceived enemy can be a person or group in our own nation or other nations.

People rarely are instructed in the ways of

peace. What we mainly are shown by writings, media and entertainment is a world in crisis and prone to aggression. Our culture gives us nearly no models for how to live in harmony with others or to move toward common solutions. So we are left with the impression that there are enemies everywhere and that the only path to peace is their destruction.

The institutions that represent us on the world stage — our countries and organizations that connect our nations — often seem prone more to confrontation than communication. Representatives at the United Nations, the World Trade Organization and others in the role of making our world work better often advocate for their member countries rather than for what works best for the whole.

But the real world is beyond the segments into which we have divided it. Humans everywhere want to be recognized as the valuable individuals they are. When each of us advocates for that to happen — hopefully by leaders of our nations and international organizations — we are more likely to move toward a world that supports solutions to the needs of everyone, including ourselves. When we insist that our leaders work toward a better planet for us to live in they will represent all of its inhabitants rather than seeking solutions based on the artificially divided world we have created.

Our planet moves forward at its own pace regardless of us and our needs. Its evolution is more long-term than our own. Our lives are but a moment in geologic time. When we honor and respect the world we honor all its inhabitants, including ourselves, and when we dishonor it we ultimately harm ourselves. Acting on that understanding can move us past the polarities into which we divide the world and can replace our momentum toward mutual destruction with that of restoration.

The forms we hold in our minds for how the world — and its people — should be block us from actually seeing it and working in concert to meet our needs. But nature only can be comprehended by long and patient observation, and even then our words and formulas will be incomplete, so we always will be working toward a more comprehensive model.[50]

We live in fear that no matter what we do, things will go wrong and that often is the case. But what happens usually is neither good nor bad in itself; what causes our dismay is perpetually dwelling on what we see as the shortcomings of others and our world. The alternative is to humbly accept the world we are given and appreciate

the life we are able to live, then moving forward as best we can with our fellow imperfect
humans. This essentially is our way of being
when we come from a place of love.

In every moment — including this one — we
can open ourselves to the feeling we seek and
then expand that to our groups, nations, and the
entire world. That will provide the guidance
we need to preserve it and its inhabitants. As in
any relationship, we can remain discontented or
accept the ways of our world. The only time we
can do this — in our interactions with individuals and on the world stage — is now.

In the Fury of the Moment
I Can See the Master's Hand[51]
– BOB DYLAN

7. THE UNIVERSE

When pondering the nature of our universe, most of us, including our scientists, admit the limits of our understanding. The evidence points to the universe as we know it starting in one place and then expanding outward, continuing in an ongoing thrust through and beyond our own time.

Our space probes provide insight into the reaches of the vast expanse around us that we only are beginning to comprehend. Many scientists believe there may be more universes beyond what we can picture.[52] Some speculate as to why matter even exists. Is everything that happens preordained or is it a product of the randomness of nature? As best we can tell, the laws we have discovered that apply to the tiny part of the cosmos in which we dwell also apply to the vast reaches beyond our current vision and imagination.[53]

Current evidence indicates a consistent story

of our origin. After the advent of our universe about 14 billion years ago, the solar system appeared 10 billion years later as the planets began to circle our sun.[54] Life, which requires self-duplication of cells, began on the earth about 3.5 billion years ago, and slowly evolved from one-cell forms using some of the elements that make up the planet, including hydrogen, carbon, nitrogen, and oxygen.[55]

We and the earth thus are intimately connected. Our water, food and air come to us via a circular system that nourishes us and to which we contribute as part of a never-ending cycle. We are one with the earth and — ultimately — the universe from which it came. This is not a mystical view but the reality of our existence.

The universe, since its inception, has engendered the creation of space, time and the objects that define it. But our concepts of that process reflect more about the nature of our minds than the universe itself. What we see — the objects and people that appear to us — exist for us because we hold a picture of them in our minds.[56] Our view is based on our need to divide the universe into parts so we can label them. This has enhanced our understanding but limits our ability to see the totality around us, which is the ongoing flow through time of interconnected objects.

The thrust of the universe is a forward movement with no name, although we have many names to describe what is in it. The founders of some religions sought to make us aware of the interconnectedness of everything in nature and taught us not to name it. God has no name in Judaism, and in Buddhism the word Dharma refers to that interconnectedness and its implication for our lives.

There is one part of our nature common to all humans. We seek knowledge to help improve our lives and aid us in our struggle for survival. From our days in caves we accumulated knowledge that has resulted in our dominance over the earth. We want to continue to learn from experience to guide us as we strive to make our lives more comfortable, and perhaps more meaningful.

But our concepts from the past don't reliably predict the future. Even in our everyday lives certainty is difficult to achieve. When we set our plans for the day we don't know if the weather will cooperate, or the traffic, or other people, or even our own moods. What seems certain is that we often will be surprised; an unexpected glitch will appear that defies our expectations no matter how detailed our plans.

In all times people have thought they know

the truth, and with truth comes a kind of immortality. Our model has gone from the geocentric view championed by ancient philosophers and medieval religions, to the certainty provided by the laws of Newton, to the relativity of Einstein, to the "uncertainty principle" of quantum mechanics, to the speculation that it all may be held together by miniscule vibrating "strings" as proposed by superstring theory.[57] But we still remain uncertain about the force that governs it all.[58]

In addition to the knowledge we need to help us manage our lives, we want to know our place in the universe. During the time humans have inhabited the earth our self-knowledge has expanded, but we still struggle to answer major questions that many of us contemplate, such as: "What is our essential nature and, if that exists, how can we get to know it?" "Are we time-limited beings or do we perpetuate our existence through our progeny and ideas?" "Is there a meaning to our existence, or do we live meaningless lives and then die, soon to be forgotten?"[59]

Considering the vastness of the universe and how much we have yet to discover — even here on earth — it seems likely there is more we don't know than we do know.[60 61] Perhaps the universe is telling us: "Be not so haughty, for as much as you think you know, you only possess a little knowledge and not much wisdom. Although you have uncovered many of my secrets, explored the cosmos and cured many diseases, there still is little you really know."

So it seems possible, with Socrates[62], that despite our constantly changing theories we actually know nothing. We continually make discoveries that lead to new perspectives, some of which contradict our previous views, and that may always be the case. And much of the advanced technology we do possess threatens mass destruction rather than improving human lives.

Perhaps our quest for knowledge reflects our desire to validate ourselves and confirm that we are worthy of love. We also hope for relationships with others to bring us fulfillment. Then we imagine that our work or recreational activities will bring the satisfaction we seek. But no amount of knowledge or interaction or activities can bring us what we most want. We hope to return to the deep feeling and involvement in life we believe we once had, but tire of trying to discover the understanding, relationship, or activity that can at last make our lives whole. Our quest — in its many forms — fails to provide that which we most seek, which is the experience of love.

We each start life with a universal perspective and soon sacrifice that view to learn the skills we need. Throughout our lives we experience a polarity between seeing ourselves as separate and as part of what is around us. Our lives become a struggle between our assumed identity and our true nature. We need to act from the view of separateness to perpetuate ourselves and the human race, and our idea of who we are dominates our lives. But our true nature remains our interconnectedness and continual interaction with all that is around us. That means that in a very real way we not only are part of — but are — the universe.

If we remind ourselves to keep our real nature in mind as we go about our daily activities, we can come to understand that we already are where we want to be, which is in a connected relationship with everything and everyone. There is nothing we need do to establish that connection. Divisions between us and what is out there are creations of our minds.

Going back to our desire to understand the universe and base our actions on that knowledge, we don't always have — and probably never will have — a clear guide for action to enable us to always know what course is wrong or right. The best framework in which we can operate is that which allows us to acknowledge and maintain our sense of connection to others and the universe.

Our main obstacle to experiencing love is our inclination to focus on everyday tasks with the hope that people and activities will bring us the connection that already is there. We distract ourselves by thinking our goal always is in the future, or that we need to obtain it somewhere outside ourselves.

Because we are part of the ongoing movement of the universe and the connection of all that is in it, love is our default view. It is our most essential self that we have been taught to sacrifice in our struggle for survival and recognition. The real universe is not one made of separate people and things. The real universe is one of connection. But our words tell us otherwise.

Our greatest books and theories — our religions, philosophies and everyday contemplations — try to bring us awareness of the universal identity that already is our nature. No efforts — and no words — can bring us to the place of love we seek because we already are there.

The connection of everything in the universe began with the advent of time and continues through this moment and beyond. The feeling of love within us cannot help being aroused when we experience the real nature of the universe and our interconnection. That understanding is what we came in with and it remains the essence of who we are. But that understanding also includes acknowledging the limits of the human identity we assume.

Universality is our most essential nature. We suffer as we deny that reality in our minds and actions, which results in eternal seeking when it already is who we are. We spend our lives seeking connection with others and all that is around us to bring us a sense of love, but that connection already is established and cannot be undone. All that is left is for each of us, if we wish, to acknowledge it.

Targeted love — of some people, places or things — leaves us feeling incomplete because it limits our experience of love to objects and situations that inevitably fall short. But opening to our connectedness is how we experience our essential loving nature. Experiencing love is not in the hands of others or the circumstances of our lives. We have the ability to allow it to ourselves in this moment and every moment. From this view there is no other way we should be; in fact, there is no other way we can be in this moment.

Being human, we will continue to be disappointed and disillusioned by what life brings.

There is much worth fighting for to move our world and lives closer to the way we want them to be. But even if we could have the ideal world we seek today, our nature that focuses on what is missing still would keep us from experiencing satisfaction.

So changing our lives and world cannot get us what we really want. It is our choice whether to allow ourselves the feeling we most seek in this moment, and the next.

If we are realistic, we expect the unexpected in our daily lives. Traumas, tragedies and catastrophes will come our way despite the relative comfort of the civilizations in which most of us dwell. The pain we experience is a reflection of the chaos of the universe. It is the rule rather than the exception.

We are myopic. We see the universe through biased eyes based on past experience. Our science expands our horizons to provide a more accurate view that we still see through the prejudices of our culture and time. A small example: nothing we encounter is a mile or inch long, or a kilometer or centimeter, yet we refer to those distances because we force our experience into pre-conceived categories we readily can understand. No one fits into the ideas we hold in our minds of white, black or brown; the skin of each individual is a different shade beyond our categories. We continually are expanding the sexual identities with which people identify. Yet many scientists once claimed that blacks are inferior and people who don't fit into traditional categories of male or female have a mental disease. The physical reality of every person — including us — is an ever-changing yet unique entity in continual interaction with the universe. Yet we rely on standards and measurements and concepts to make communication possible. They allow us to function, but mask the reality in front of us.

Although we need the categories into which we cast everything and everyone to allow us to function, we can acknowledge their limits to ourselves and among us. We can extend empathy to appreciate what is on the inside of people as well as the outside. We can ask questions that allow others to reveal their interests, hopes and beliefs. We can encounter people with appreciation. And as we do this we experience the appreciation we seek.

As long as we think we are incomplete or inadequate, that will be our experience. But love is our most essential self. The real world — that both flows through us and encompasses us — is not one of separateness, but one of connection. There is a part of us that knows that, which we have learned to distrust. But in this moment — and every moment — we can remember that view. We can allow our essential self to reemerge in our feelings and thoughts, then bring who we really are into our actions.

We miss the active involvement with the universe that we knew from our earliest moments, but we can reignite that perspective by acknowledging the good in people and engaging fully in life even as we concede how little we know. We can commit ourselves to learning from engagement with everyone and everything we encounter. When our view of the universe is opening and widening, our minds and spirits come alive. We don't need to wait for fulfillment to come to us. We can experience what we most want as we extend our sense of connection to others and all that surrounds us.

The deep feeling to which we seek to return supersedes every other aspect of our lives. We usually think of it as tied to a person or situation. But there is nothing we need to do. That feeling comes to us when we simply open our minds and hearts and allow it in. The most essential aspect of who we are already is there and awaits being reawakened. We can allow it to ourselves when we decide to unblock it, which we might just choose to do in this moment.

Our lives will continue to go in directions different from what we imagined. The universe is not designed to meet our expectations and there can be no certainty of what it will bring. But when in tune with our oneness with the universe we see that all is moving in the inexorable direction it always has and always will. And, if we choose, we can humbly accept what it provides as a gift for which we offer infinite thanks.

We started by simply observing all that surrounds us, not knowing who we are. And still, who we really are is not the self, other person, group, nation or world, but the one who continually observes. Our essence is consciousness itself — what some call the soul — while our body is ever-changing in its interaction with the universe. Our real nature is beyond the descriptions provided by our words, but best can be understood by the continual process of observation. Our real self never dies or goes away. We only can approach understanding it as we engage in the encounters of every ongoing moment of our lives.

NOTES

1 Quoted in *The Path to Paradise*, Sam Wasson, Page 137.

2 *Civilization and Its Discontents*, Sigmund Freud, Page 13: "Originally the ego includes everything, later it detaches itself from the external world."

3 *Louder than Words*, Benjamin Bergen, Page 25: "When we visualize actions – consciously and intentionally activating mental images – we use the very parts of our brain that control our body's movements."

4 *Breath*, James Nestor, Page 211: "People with anxiety...could unwittingly be holding their breath throughout the day."

5 *Surviving our Catastrophes*, Robert Jay Lifton, Page 4: "A victim can feel immobilized psychically as well as physically, preoccupied with his or her misfortune."

6 *Civilization and Its Discontents*, Sigmund Freud, Page 37: "I am speaking of that way of life which makes love the center of all things and anticipates all happiness from loving and being loved."

7 *Excellent Sheep, The Miseducation of the American Elite*, William Deresiewicz, Page 8: "Look beneath the façade of affable confidence and seamless well-adjustment that today's elite students have learned to project, and what you often find are toxic levels of fear, anxiety, and depression, of emptiness and aimlessness and isolation."

8 *Brain Study Suggests Traumatic Memories Are Processed as Present Experience*, Ellen Barry, New York Times, November 20, 2023: "Traumatic memories had their own neural mechanism, brain scans showed, which may help explain their vivid and intrusive nature."

9 *Behave,* Robert M. Sapolsky, Page 28: "The cortex is where muscles are commanded to move, where language is comprehended and produced, where memories are stored, where spatial and mathematical skills reside, where executive decisions are made."

10 From *Because of You* by Arthur Hammerstein and Dudley Wilkinson, 1940.

11 *My Life After Hate*, Arno Michaelis, Page 31: "Hate takes a terrible toll on life. Fear is indeed the mind-killer. ...You will find what you are looking for, so think deeply about what you seek."

12 *A study of ancient Japanese bones might challenge our ideas about human nature*, Sarah Kaplan, Washington Post, April 1, 2016: "The grotesque tableau, discovered in Nataruk, Kenya, is the oldest known evidence of prehistoric warfare, scientists said in the journal Nature earlier this year. The scattered, scrambled remains of 27 men, women and children seemed to illustrate that conflict is not simply a symptom of our modern sedentary societies and expansionist ambitions....And yet, for all the evidence that warfare is a deep and ancient aspect of human behavior, there are also signs that it may not be an inevitable one. Another group of ancient skeletons from the other side of the world tells a different story: One about humans who had the capacity for violence, but refrained."

13 Nazis were known as being excellent family men. This has been portrayed in such films as *Schindler's List and The Zone of Interest.*

14 *Behave*, Robert Sapolsky, Page 523: "Compassion [is] where your resonance with someone's distress leads you to actually help."

15 *On Aggression*, Conrad Lorenz, Page 50: "Lack of social contact, and above all deprivation of it, [are] among the factors strongly predisposing [us] to facilitate aggression."

16 Ex-Pittsburg mayor's journey to forgiveness after son's stabbing death.

https://www.mercurynews.com/2023/12/31/a-former-pittsburg-mayor-suffered-in-silence-after-his-son-was-mortally-wounded-in-a-stabbing-his-long-journey-ended-with-forgiveness-compassion/

17 *The Power of Habit*, Charles Duhigg, 2012, Page 25: "We might not remember the experiences that create our habits, but once they are lodged in our brains they influence how we act – often without our realization."

18 *How to Know a Person*, David Brooks, Page 154.

19 *Fatal Invention*, Dorothy Roberts, Page 4: "Race is not a biological category that is politically charged. It is a political category that has been disguised as a biological one....There are no human populations with such a high degree of genetic differentiation that they objectively fall into races."

20 *The Origins of Political Order*, Francis Fukuyama, Page 53: "For bands and tribes, social organization is based on kinship, and these societies are relatively egalitarian."

21 Anna Michailidou, I.B Dogan, 2008: "Trading in prehistory and protohistory: Perspectives from the eastern Aegean and beyond – Part 1."

22 https://study.com/academy/lesson/rhesus-macaque-monkey-lifespan-behavior-facts.html

23 *My Life After Hate*, Arno Michaelis, Page 34: "I was drawn to racist ideology because I felt like white people were getting shafted. We were the underdogs. It was us against the world in an epic battle for forever."

24 George Washington, *Farewell Address*, 1796: "There is an opinion that parties in free countries are useful checks upon the administration of the government and serve to keep alive the spirit of liberty.... But in those of the popular character, in governments purely elective, it is a spirit not to be encouraged."

25 *Talking to the Ground*, Douglas Preston, Page 291: "A powerful elite...used cannibalism in the Southwest as a form of social control – to frighten, intimidate, and subjugate people."

26 *The Landmark Thucydides*, 1.113.1: "Athenians... took Chaeronea, made slaves of the inhabitants, and leaving a garrison, commenced their return."

27 https://www.britannica.com/science/confirmation-bias

28 One of the few books that discusses consciousness from a scientific viewpoint is *Conscious*, by Annaka A. Harris. Page 5: "It's this simple difference – whether there is experience present or not – which we can all use as a reference point, that constitutes what I mean by the word 'consciousness.'" Erich Neumann also wrote a classic from the Jungian perspective, *The Origins and History of Consciousness*.

Page 6: "The beginning can be laid hold of in two 'places:' it can be conceived in the life of mankind as the earliest dawn of human history, and in the life of the individual as the earliest dawn of childhood.... In all people, and in all religions, creation appears as the creation of light."

29 From the song *Russians*, 1985.

30 In patriotic tributes to the United States, for example, the terms are used interchangeably. *The Pledge of Allegiance* mentions: "One Nation under God," while there also is the popular song: "*My Country 'Tis of Thee.*"

31 *The Fortunes of Africa*, Martin Meredith, Page 637: "A new breed of dictators emerged [early 1990s], adept at maintaining a veneer of democracy sufficient for them to be able to obtain foreign aid."

32 *The Nature of Prejudice*, Gordon W. Allport, Page 20 "The human mind must think with the aid of categories (or generalizations). Once formed, categories are the basis for normal prejudgment. We cannot possibly avoid this process. Orderly living depends on it."

33 *Thinking Fast and Slow*, Daniel Kahneman, Pages 20-21: "System 1 operates automatically and quickly, with little or no effort and no sense of voluntary control...System 2 allocates attention to the effortful mental activities that demand it, including complex computations."

34 *Behave*, Robert Sapolsky, Page 291: "Hunter-gatherer societies have typically been egalitarian... Inequality emerged following animal domestication and the development of agriculture. The more stuff... the greater the potential inequality."

35 "A Nation is a Nation, is a State, Is an Ethnic Group," Walker Conner, In *Nationalism*, Page 36, edited by John Hutchinson and Anthony D. Smith.

36 "Nationalism and High Culture," Ernest Gellner, In *Nationalism*, Page 64, edited by John Hutchinson and Anthony D. Smith.

37 *Fascism – A Warning*, Madeleine Albright, Page 245: "We need to work well with others, whether we are trying to stop terrorists, preserve the environment, halt the spread of nuclear arms, raise living standards, prevent epidemic disease, put international drug dealers in jail, or safeguard our borders."

38 Screenplay by Greta Gerwig and Noah Baumbach.

39 The completion of the Human Genome Project in 2003 confirmed humans are 99.9% identical at the DNA level and there is no genetic basis for race. National Institutes of Health (NIH) (.gov)

https://www.ncbi.nlm.nih.gov › articles › PMC8604262

40 *The Body Keeps the Score*, Bessel Van Der Kolk, Page 75: "We instinctively read the dynamic between two people simply from their tension or relaxation, their posture and tone of voice, their changing facial expressions."

41 *Lost Connections*, Johann Hari, Page 93: "You and I exist for one reason – because those humans figured out how to cooperate. They shared their food. They looked after the sick. They were able to take down large beasts only because they were working together."

42 *Albert Einstein, Philosopher Scientist*, Edited by Paul Arthur Schilpp, Page 13: "All concepts, even

those that are closest to experience, are from the point of view of logic freely chosen conventions." Einstein is saying that we create the concepts by which we see the world to aid our understanding.

43 *Power and Governance in a Partially Globalized World*, Robert O. Keohane, Page 17.

44 *Civilization and Its Discontents*, Sigmund Freud, Page 102: "The tendency to aggression is an innate, independent, instinctual disposition in man, and...it constitutes the most powerful obstacle to culture."

45 *On Aggression*, Conrad Lorenz, Page 42: "The aggression drive, still a hereditary evil of mankind, is the consequence of a process of intra-specific selection which worked on our forefathers for roughly forty thousand years."

46 *Why We Cooperate*, Michael Tomasello, Page XIII: "We may refer to the underlying psychological processes that make these unique forms of cooperation possible as 'shared intentionality.' "

47 *Brighter Climate Futures*, Hari Lamba, Page 19: "Global warming is not some distant future problem. It has already begun to devastate the US and the world...when air temperature rises, there is greater evaporation from the sun, and the air has more energy. This leads to two effects: it increases the energy and hence the wind velocity of weather related phenomenon like hurricanes, tornadoes, coastal storms, while increasing the amount or rain most of the time."

48 See note #24 above.

49 *Ancient Scythians used human skin for leather, confirming Herodotus' grisly claim.*

https://www.livescience.com/archaeology/ancient-scythians-used-human-skin-for-leather-confirming-herodotus-grisly-claim

50 *The Structure of Scientific Revolutions*, Thomas Kuhn, Page 6: "Scientific revolutions...necessitated the [scientific] community's rejection of time-honored scientific theory in favor of another incompatible with it." (Meaning: Our models of nature change when new discoveries force us to do so.)

51 From the song *Every Grain of Sand*, 1981.

52 "*A Universe from Nothing*, Lawrence Krauss, Page 142: "It is now traditional to think of 'our' universe as comprising simply the totality of all we can now see and all that we could ever see. The minute one chooses this definition for a universe, the possibility of other 'universes'...becomes possible."

53 *A Universe from Nothing*, Lawrence Krauss, Page 126: "A universe from nothing...that arises naturally, and even inevitably, is increasingly consistent with everything we have learned about the world."

54 *The Story of Earth*, Robert M. Hazen, Page 7: "Our solar system, with its glowing central star and varied planet and moons, is a relative newcomer to the cosmos – a mere 4.5 billion years old...The moment of creation remains the most elusive, incomprehensible, defining event in the history of the universe."

55 *The Story of Earth*, Robert M. Hazen, Page 149: "A few of Earth's most ancient sedimentary rocks, those laid down in shallow ocean environments about 3.5 billion years ago, hold unmistakable microbial fossils."

56 In a collection of his essays, *Ecrits*, Page 65, the great French psychoanalyst Jacque Lacan states that

our "concepts engender [create] things," rather than the other way around.

57 *The Fabric of the Cosmos*, Brian Greene, Page 78: "Every age develops its story or metaphor for how the universe was conceived and structured."

58 *A Brief History of Time*, Stephen Hawking, Page 140: "If we discover a complete theory, it should in time be understandable by everyone, not just by a few scientists. Then we shall all, philosophers, scientists and just ordinary people, be able to take part in the discussion of the question of why it is that we and the universe exists. If we find the answer to that, it would be the ultimate triumph of human reason – for then we should know the mind of God."

59 *The Denial of Death*, Ernest Becker, Page 5: "Our hope and belief is that the things that man creates are of lasting worth and meaning, that they outlive death and decay."

60 A new scientific discovery documented on the pages of the Washington Post: "How did life on Earth begin? The chemical puzzle just became clearer."

https://www.washingtonpost.com/climate-environment/2024/02/29/life-earth-origin-chemistry/

61 An article about new species being discovered off the coast of Chile: "See the dozens of new species this deep-sea robot just discovered." https://www.washingtonpost.com/climate-environment/2024/02/24/new-species-deep-sea/

62 *Plato's Republic*, Section 354: "Socrates: Hence the result of the discussion, as far as I'm concerned, is that I know nothing, for when I don't know what justice is I'll hardly know whether it is a kind of virtue or not, or whether a person who has it is happy or unhappy."

BOOKS USED FOR REFERENCE

Albert Einstein, Philosopher Scientist, Edited by Paul Arthur Schilpp, 1949, Library of Living Philosophers.

Behave, Robert M. Sapolsky, 2018, Penguin.

The Body Keeps the Score: Brain, Mind and Body in the Healing of Trauma, Bessel Van Der Kolk, 2014, Penguin.

Breath: The New Science of a Lost Art, James Nestor, 2020, Riverhead Books.

A Brief History of Time, Stephen Hawking, 1988, Bantam.

Brighter Climate Futures, Hari Lamba, 2020, Regent Press.

Civilization and Its Discontents, Sigmund Freud, 2011, Martino Publishing, Originally published 1930.

Conscious, Annaka Harris, Harper, 2019.

The Cultural Origins of Human Cognition, Michael Tomasello, 1999, Harvard University Press.

The Denial of Death, Ernest Becker, 1973, Free Press.

Excellent Sheep: The Miseducation of the American Elite and the Way to a Meaningful Life, William Deresiewicz, 2014, Free Press.

The Fabric of the Cosmos: Time, Space and the Texture of Reality, Brian Greene, 2005, Vintage.

Fascism – A Warning, Madeleine Albright, 2018, Harper Perennial.

Fatal Invention, Dorothy Roberts, 2011, The New Press.

The Fortunes of Africa, Martin Meredith, 2014, Public Affairs.

How to Know a Person: The Art of Seeing Others Deeply and Being Deeply Seen, David Brooks, 2023, Random House.

The Landmark Thucydides: A Comprehensive Guide to the Peloponnesian War, Edited by Robert B. Strassler, 1996, Free Press.

Lost Connections: Why You're Depressed and How to Find Hope, Johann Hari, 2019, Bloomsbury.

My Life After Hate, Arno Michaelis, 2012, Authentic Presence Publications.

Louder than Words, Ben K. Bergen, 2014, Basic Books.

Nationalism, Edited by John Hutchinson and Anthony D. Smith, 2012, Oxford University Press.

The Nature of Prejudice, Gordon W. Allport, 1979, Perseus.

On Aggression, Conrad Lorenz, 1966, Harcourt.

The Origins and History of Consciousness, Erich Neumann, 1973, Bollingen.

The Origins of Political Order: From Prehuman Times to the French Revolution, Francis Fukuyama, 2011, Farrar, Straus and Giroux.

The Path to Paradise, Sam Wasson, 2023, Harper Collins.

Plato's Republic, 2007, Penguin.

Power and Governance in a Partially Globalized World, Robert O. Keohane, 2002, Routledge.

The Power of Habit, Charles Duhigg, 2012, Random House.

The Story of Earth, Robert M. Hazen, 2013, Penguin.

The Structure of Scientific Revolutions, Thomas Kuhn, 2012, University of Chicago Press.

Surviving our Catastrophes, Robert Jay Lifton, 2023, The New Press.

Talking to the Ground, Douglas Preston, 2019, Simon and Schuster.

Thinking Fast and Slow, Daniel Kahneman, 2013, Farrar, Straus and Giroux.

A Universe from Nothing, Lawrence Krauss, 2013, Atria.

Why We Cooperate, Michael Tomasello, 2009, MIT Press.

About the Author

Steve Zolno graduated from Shimer College with a bachelor's degree in Social Sciences and holds a master's in Educational Psychology from Sonoma State University. Steve has founded and directed private schools and a health care agency in the San Francisco Bay Area.

Printed in the USA
CPSIA information can be obtained
at www.ICGtesting.com
LVHW090721030624
782094LV00005B/72